# My School

By Manuel Ruiz

Scott Foresman
is an imprint of

Glenview, Illinois • Boston, Massachusetts • Mesa, Arizona
Shoreview, Minnesota • Upper Saddle River, New Jersey

ISBN 13: 978-0-328-39736-5
ISBN 10:     0-328-39736-9

This is my school bus.

This is my school.

This is my playground.

This is my desk.

This is my teacher.

This is my class.